Contents

KT-362-958

Introduction

People have been writing about time management for at least 800 years. Of course times change, but finding enough time in the day to get everything done has always been a challenge. When St Marher wrote in 1225 that 'Time and tide wait for no man', he did not have phones ringing or emails pinging. But he clearly recognized the problem we all have getting things done. Most of us still find it virtually impossible to clear our desk by the end of each day. We all over-commit, struggle to prioritize and allow ourselves to be distracted.

Much more recently, Douglas Adams (author of *The Hitchhiker's Guide to the Galaxy*) wrote that he loved 'the whoosh deadlines made as they rushed by'. In other words, he found it almost impossible to start a task until it was almost too late to complete it on time. I bet you can relate to that phenomenon – I know I can.

Perhaps like you, I find it difficult to say no to things. I underestimate how long things really take to do and waste time on doomed projects, just in case I can turn them round. My wife says I'm a soft touch and that people take advantage. She's probably right and, yes, the truth can hurt, but sometimes we all need to be told it like it is. I hope you have someone in your life who can talk to you in the same way.

Looking back over my career, I can see countless examples of how I could have managed my time better. I'm sure I could have achieved more success sooner, had I made better use of my time. Even more importantly, I am convinced I failed to make the best use of the people around me. It took me years to realize that what matters most is getting the job done – not that it is done my way, by me alone.

Successful Time Management

Robert Ashton

www.inaweek.co.uk

Teach Yourself®

IN A WEEK

Hodder Education

338 Euston Road, London NW1 3BH.

Hodder Education is an Hachette UK company

First published in UK 2012 by Hodder Education

This edition published 2012.

Copyright © 2012 Robert Ashton

The moral rights of the author have been asserted

Database right Hodder Education (makers)

The *Teach Yourself* name is a registered trademark of Hachette UK.

British Library Cataloguing in Publication Data: a catalogue record for this title is available from the British Library.

The publisher has used its best endeavours to ensure that any website addresses referred to in this book are correct and active at the time of going to press. However, the publisher and the author have no responsibility for the websites and can make no guarantee that a site will remain live or that the content will remain relevant, decent or appropriate.

The publisher has made every effort to mark as such all words which it believes to be trademarks. The publisher should also like to make it clear that the presence of a word in the book, whether marked or unmarked, in no way affects its legal status as a trademark.

Every reasonable effort has been made by the publisher to trace the copyright holders of material in this book. Any errors or omissions should be notified in writing to the publisher, who will endeavour to rectify the situation for any reprints and future editions.

Hachette UK's policy is to use papers that are natural, renewable and recyclable products and made from wood grown in sustainable forests. The logging and manufacturing processes are expected to conform to the environmental regulations of the country of origin.

www.hoddereducation.co.uk

Typeset by Cenveo Publisher Services.

Printed in Great Britain by CPI Group (UK) Ltd, Croydon, CR0 4YY.

I learned time management the hard way. I have written this book to make it easier for you, for the simple reason that none of those I've read to date has really helped me. Some are too long and some are, frankly, too short. Some focus entirely on techniques, when attitude is clearly just as important.

What I've tried to do here is to write the book I know I needed to read. I hope reading it does as much for you as writing it has done for me.

Robert Ashton

SUNDAY

It all starts with you

Today we're going to think about you. You are the most important person in the whole time management equation. Furthermore, you are different from me and everyone else because each of us is unique. No two people have the same mix of ability, aspiration, interests and experience.

We'll start by encouraging you to reflect on where you find yourself in the world today and where you plan to go tomorrow. Life is, as they say, a journey and today we're going to map the next stage of the trip. A simple principle we need to explore is that the more you want to do something, the faster and better you'll do it.

We also need to take a look at how you work best. Are you a lark or an owl? Does your boss give you the freedom to plan your time or does work seem an endless treadmill? You might feel in control, or you might feel completely overwhelmed, in which case we need to help you dig yourself out from your work pile.

Today you're going to find answers to three questions:

- Where do I really want to go?
- How do I work best?
- What's holding me back?

Where are you going?

In one of the most famous speeches of the 20th century, civil rights activist Martin Luther King said, 'I have a dream.' He was a powerful speaker because he had such a clear vision of what he wanted to bring about: the end of racial discrimination in the USA. His speeches are still remembered, even though he died almost 50 years ago.

Political campaigners are often single-minded like Martin Luther King. They devote all their time and energy to a single cause, often regardless of the risk. You, on the other hand, may not have a cause you feel strongly enough to die for, but that doesn't mean you cannot be passionate, single-minded and determined. Only when you know what you want from life can you go out and get it.

'You never achieve success unless you like what you are doing.'
Dale Carnegie

Define your dream

Your dream is every bit as important to you as Martin Luther King's dream was to him. No one person's dream is better than another's. All dreams are equal. What you need to have, though, is a crystal-clear vision of your dream. It needs to be something that you can see, feel and know – deep down – you can achieve.

Although it's good to be ambitious, your dream also needs to be realistic. Very few people achieve immense wealth, global fame or rise through the ranks to lead a large organization. The truth is that few actually want to. In fact, some people simply want to stay as they are, but feel more in control of their lives.

Ask yourself these questions and start to define your dream.

● In five/ten years' time what do I want to spend most of my time doing?
● What appeals most to me about this?
● What path do I need to follow to realize my dream?

Case study

Wendy worked in the office at her local primary school. Her father had been a baker and every term she taught a group of pupils how to make bread. She loved working at the school, but was becoming increasingly disenchanted with the growing volume of paperwork. She looked at the three questions above and wrote the following answers.

- In five years' time I want to be working with the children every day.

- What I like best is their excitement when they learn something new.

- To work in the classroom I need to qualify as a teaching assistant, then perhaps do teacher training later.

Wendy found a suitable course and, to her surprise, the school offered to fund it for her. Within a year she was working in the classroom and had started teacher training.

The length and difficulty of the journey to your dream will depend on its magnitude and complexity. As you can see from the case study, Wendy took her ambition one step at a time. She might eventually become a head teacher, but sensibly she started by training to work in the classroom. Working with youngsters was her dream.

> **TIP** *The sooner you can spend more time doing what you enjoy at work, the more motivated you will be and the more you will achieve.*

How do you work best?

We all work in different ways, and function best when in tune with our body clock. For example, you might:

- prefer to be outside in all weathers or enjoy always being indoors in the warm
- be happier as a member of a large team or prefer to work on your own
- feel more productive at 8 a.m. or at your best at midnight
- enjoy the freedom to decide what needs doing or perform well only once you have been given a detailed task list each morning.

Few of us have the luxury of total choice over how we work. Even the best jobs have less enjoyable aspects. If you were a bus driver, for example, you may have chosen the job because you enjoy driving and meeting people. Cleaning the bus at the end of the day or checking the oil are less pleasurable, but no less important. We all have to accept aspects of our work that we don't really enjoy. Some tasks you just have to get on and do.

A flexible working day

You will already know how you work best, although you might not have thought about how you can flex your working day to accommodate your body clock. If you're lucky, your company gives you the flexibility to start early or finish late, depending on your preference. Even if this is not possible, you can adapt your working routine so that you undertake the most important tasks when you are at your most alert.

Let's start by dividing the day into quarters. Then look at how differently a morning or afternoon person might choose to spend their day.

Time of day	Morning person (lark)	Afternoon person (owl)
Early morning	• Priority task	• Priority list for the day • Routine tasks
Late morning	• Secondary task	• Secondary task
Lunchtime		
Early afternoon	• Admin or meetings	• Admin or meetings
Late afternoon	• Routine tasks • Priority list for tomorrow	• Priority task

You'll see from the table that morning people:

● start the day with the most important task
● end the day listing the next day's priorities.

Evening people, however:

● start the day listing the day's priorities
● end the day with the most important task.

TIP *If you work best in the morning, try going in to work an hour early so you're in full flow when your colleagues arrive. Then take a long lunch break.*

Schedule your time

The last section introduced a couple of concepts we'll explore in more detail on Wednesday. These are prioritizing tasks and breaking the day down into chunks.

Priority tasks are those that are most important to you right now. This might be because they are crucial to your job, or because you have been putting them off and the deadline is fast approaching. These are the tasks you focus on when most alert and able to give them your best.

Breaking the day into chunks is a great way to pace your working time. It makes it easier to work on one task at a time without worrying about what's being neglected, because you have scheduled your time and know what you'll be working on when.

There are two things you need to know if you are to schedule your time:

- how much time you have
- how long each task will take to complete.

A diary will enable you to set aside blocks of time for specific tasks. You will also need to give each task a time estimate. Keeping a timesheet will enable you to record how you actually spend your time. This is important as most people underestimate how long a task will take. They then feel they are very busy but not achieving much. Does that sound familiar to you? It certainly does to me!

Case study

Rupesh hated mornings. At university, life had been fine, but now he was expected to be in the office by nine. What's more, every morning seemed to start with an argument with his boss about what he had not finished the day before.

Rupesh worked in housing and his job was to investigate and respond to enquiries too complicated for colleagues on the help desk to answer straight away. The problem was that people expected to be called back the next morning with an answer, and he was always juggling tasks.

What Rupesh needed was a couple of hours a day to research the complicated cases and write them up without distraction. Starting the day off with a backlog was not helping anyone.

Rupesh discussed the problem with his manager, who agreed to let him come in at 10.30 in the morning and stay until 6.30 in the evening. This gave him some quality time after his colleagues had gone home and meant he could lie in each morning. Because he worked best late in the day, his productivity soared and so did his mood.

Understand what holds you back

If you've read any self-help books, you'll know that defining your dreams and vision for the future is important. You'll also know that what usually gets between you and achieving those dreams is you. The same applies to making best use of your time. To put it simply, good time management means doing what you consider important when you feel best able to do it.

Even if you work on your own, this can be difficult. The problem is that most of us are far too nice for our own good. Our work efficiency and effectiveness suffer because we allow other people to divert us from our priorities. On Thursday we'll look at some techniques to help you avoid distraction, but today we're thinking about you. Two of the things that might be holding you back from managing your time well are lack of self-confidence and lack of motivation.

Boost self-confidence

If you doubt your ability or value, so will others. If, on the other hand, you have total self-belief, many people will take you at your word and assume that you can do everything you say. Many factors influence our level of self-confidence. You can boost your self-confidence by:

- knowing yourself and valuing the experiences that have shaped you
- recognizing that no one can be good at everything
- not comparing yourself with others, because you'll always focus on what they do better and overlook what you do better than them
- being assertive and not letting others push you around
- not taking criticism personally, but instead treating it as advice.

Boost self-motivation

We all need to be motivated to perform well in our job. A good employer will work hard to give you the clarity of role and support you need to do well. But you also need to be

self-motivated. We are all different, and what to some might appear a dream job, might look truly awful to someone else. Motivating yourself is easier if you:

- believe in what your organization does and consider it worth while
- have not grown bored with your job and keep finding new challenges to excite you
- treat yourself when you do something really well, or complete a task you don't enjoy
- are in control of your workload rather than feeling burdened by others.

Summary

Today you were encouraged to think about your dreams and vision for your future. Only when you know where you want to go can you fully appreciate how your career can help you get there. Managing your time starts with being confident that you're doing the right thing and that, even when it's tough, the end result will make it all worth while.

We also looked at how you work best. Once you know the time of day when you are most effective, you'll appreciate the benefit of doing the most important tasks when you feel most able to cope with them. This means taking control of your working day and doing things in the order that suits you, rather than starting at the top of a list and working your way down it.

Personal factors can also get in the way of good time management. The better you feel about yourself the more you'll be able to assert yourself and feel in control of your work and life. You also need to be self-motivated by really believing in what you do for a living. When your job fits with your personal values you won't feel compromised.

SUNDAY

MONDAY

TUESDAY

WEDNESDAY

THURSDAY

FRIDAY

SATURDAY

Fact-check

1. What is a key factor of time management?
   - a) It's personal to each of us because we're all unique ❏
   - b) It's simply a matter of all of us following the same processes ❏
   - c) It's impossible to improve because life's like that ❏
   - d) It's difficult because I am just too busy ❏

2. What is Martin Luther King best remembered for?
   - a) Being really busy ❏
   - b) Not really knowing what he was trying to achieve ❏
   - c) Having a dream ❏
   - d) Being a really nice guy who always made time for people ❏

3. How should you define your own dream or vision for your future?
   - a) Remember what your mother said you should be aiming for ❏
   - b) Be able to describe clearly your life as you want it to be in five years' time ❏
   - c) Read lots of books and see what other people have done ❏
   - d) Ask your friends what they think you should be doing ❏

4. How will you be most productive at work?
   - a) By doing things you don't like ❏
   - b) By feeling uncomfortable and out of your depth ❏
   - c) By being passionate about your work, loving every minute ❏
   - d) By being given no direction and left to find your own way ❏

5. If you like mornings but get tired after lunch, how should you start the day?
   - a) By doing the most important thing you have to do ❏
   - b) By making a list of the day's tasks ❏
   - c) By chatting to colleagues ❏
   - d) With a cooked breakfast ❏

6. What will happen if you break your working day down into four two-hour chunks?
   - a) You'll find the time passes more quickly ❏
   - b) Time will seem to drag ❏
   - c) You'll constantly run out of time ❏
   - d) You'll get more done because you are scheduling your day ❏

7. What's the best way to work out how long things take you to do?
a) Buy a stopwatch ❏
b) Keep a simple paper timesheet and record what you're doing each half hour ❏
c) Ask a colleague to keep an eye on you ❏
d) Download a sophisticated time-recording package on to your PC ❏

8. If you keep a record of how long tasks take, what will you soon be able to do?
a) Demand a pay rise ❏
b) Get promoted ❏
c) Accurately schedule your working day because you know how long you take to do things ❏
d) Pick up when other people are slacking ❏

9. How can you boost your self-confidence?
a) By dressing boldly in bright colours ❏
b) By avoiding conflict because it rocks your confidence ❏
c) By recognizing what you do well and focusing on doing it well ❏
d) By blowing the whistle on the office bully ❏

10. What's an effective way to be more motivated at work?
a) To believe in your organization and what it does ❏
b) To try to pass the day by thinking about your favourite hobby ❏
c) Keeping fit and exercising at lunchtime ❏
d) Being nice to your boss so that (s)he's nice to you ❏

SUNDAY

MONDAY

TUESDAY

WEDNESDAY

THURSDAY

FRIDAY

SATURDAY

MONDAY

Understanding your job

Although you might lead a hectic social life, it's at work where time management is most likely to become an issue. There's a good reason for this. It's because at work you're being paid for your time and expertise.

We'll start by looking at your relationship with your employer. Get this right and you will feel more in control of your workload. Then we'll look at your job itself and its depth and breadth. Are you doing too much and, if so, why? We'll explore some techniques that will help you deal with this issue.

Finally, we'll look in more detail at the way we make decisions. Sitting on the fence not only hurts, but it also takes up time that you could perhaps better use to get on with the job. We'll also explore procrastination. It's something we all do, so we need to understand why it's so common and what it might mean.

Today we'll answer these questions:

- What is my job and what is not?
- How can I stop myself saying yes to my boss?
- Why are decisions so difficult to make?

Manage your job

We all spend a significant part of our lives at work. Our jobs are important to us, not least because, unless we are lucky enough to be very wealthy, we need paid employment so that we can pay our bills. This, in many ways, is the root of a common problem: many of us feel that we need our job more than our job needs us.

Of course, a lot depends on the job you do. Different kinds of job demand differing levels of commitment from those who do them. A soldier might be expected to take massive personal risks, even risk life to complete a strategically important task. A factory shift worker, on the other hand, can clock off when the whistle blows and not think about work again until the following day.

While, for most of us, our job doesn't endanger our life, it does have a habit of intruding into every aspect of our life. That is because we feel dependent upon it and even subconsciously strive to preserve it.

'Give us the tools and we'll finish the job.'

Winston Churchill

SUNDAY

MONDAY

TUESDAY

WEDNESDAY

THURSDAY

FRIDAY

SATURDAY

The truth about work

If you are paid monthly, you will receive a cheque at the end of each month for the work you've done. Then you and your employer both start the next month afresh. That is the extent of the contractual commitment you have to each other. Loyalty and respect are important, but only if mutual and equal.

Overcommitting

It is human nature to want to please. This makes it all too easy to overload your working life. No amount of time management techniques can help you squeeze two days' work into one. So here are some warning signs to look out for.

● **Are you volunteering too quickly?**
Make sure you have the time before you agree to take on additional work.

● **Are you straying from your brief?**
As you get deeper into a project, you spot other things that need to be done. Highlight them but don't assume you have to do them.

● **Are you neglecting home life?**
If you work all the time and neglect your personal life, your work quality and work rate will suffer.

And here are some ways to avoid overcommitting.

● Set aside time in your diary for recurring tasks well into the future.
● Confirm exactly what's expected of you when you take on each task.
● Book out personal time in your diary and also time to plan.

Case study

Warren's grandfather had been an ardent trade unionist during the 1970s. As Warren grew up, he'd been told about the way workers stuck to their job and their job alone. His grandfather told him this was called 'demarcation'.

When Warren's boss at the office asked him to take on extra work, he was naturally wary. He remembered how his grandfather had gone on strike rather than accept extra duties for no extra pay.

Warren tried to argue that extra work for no more pay was unfair. However, because he did not schedule or plan his working day, he had no evidence to support his case and so found himself with more work. He started scheduling his time and found his work rate increased. How times have changed, he thought to himself.

Overengineering

You have an eye for detail and want to get every last aspect of a task perfect before passing it on. Remember, however, that to most people, perfection is only a little better than good enough. Furthermore, if your work is being charged on to a client, they may not need or be willing to fund the additional detail you have provided.

Understand your boss

You can dramatically improve your time management if you improve your relationship with your manager. That's not to suggest that you don't already get on with your boss. It's more that they are probably also wrestling with their time management and delegating to you may be very convenient.

Use transactional analysis

This phrase simply refers to the power balance in a relationship. It's important here because the relationship between manager and those managed is often out of balance. That's because your manager has power over you, if only because they are higher up the organization's pecking order.

Transactional analysis teaches that there are three personality states between which we all move:

- **parent** – dominating and using behaviour learned from one's own parents
- **adult** – rational, objective and less emotional behaviour
- **child** – submissive, emotional and reactive behaviour we learned as children.

You don't need to understand the detail of transactional analysis to improve your time management. However, you do need to appreciate that:

- if you respond to your boss emotionally (child), he or she will become more dominating (parent)
- if your boss is unreasonably demanding (parent) and you respond rationally and unemotionally (adult), your boss will also become more rational (adult) and easier to negotiate with
- if you respond emotionally (child) to the demanding (parent) boss, you are far more likely to find yourself with too much to do in too little time.

SUNDAY
MONDAY
TUESDAY
WEDNESDAY
THURSDAY
FRIDAY
SATURDAY

TIP *Try to avoid responding emotionally to demands from your manager. Instead, ask a question to encourage your manager to think rationally about the wider impact of what they are suggesting. In other words, don't say, 'Oh heck, I don't have time for that.' Instead, say, 'You'll appreciate that I already have a full week. How do you suggest I juggle things to fit this extra work in?'*

Manage your boss and manage your workload

Once you have your relationship with your boss on an even footing, you can become more proactive in managing your workload. In short, you are far less likely to have extra work dumped on you. That's because you engage in adult-to-adult dialogue.

Here are some good ways to manage your boss and your workload.

- **Accept rather than challenge the way your boss is**. Work around your manager's shortcomings and recognize how you can help her or him succeed.
- **Present solutions, not problems**. This enables you to remain in control of your workload and commitment.
- **Ask for advice, not instruction**. You know what needs to be done and have planned the time to do it. Ask for advice about how, not why, when or if.
- **Be honest** and say if you feel you're being overloaded or asked to do things that are really unnecessary. Use a work plan to illustrate the problem.

TIP *Always under-promise so that you can over-deliver. For example, if you've scheduled a task for Wednesday, say it will be complete by Thursday, not Wednesday afternoon. Then you always meet agreed deadlines with time to spare.*

Be decisive

If you find it difficult to make decisions and procrastinate, time will run away with you. To be effective in how you manage your time at work, you need to be decisive. The more time you spend weighing up the options, the less time you have to follow the path you choose.

Nobody can make only correct decisions. That is because only by looking back after the event can you know whether you chose the right option. Even then, other factors might have also changed so that you can never be certain your decision was the best. All you can do is make your decision based on the situation as it appeared at the time.

Things to avoid

The more you can avoid or manage these behavioural traits, the more decisive you will be:

● **needing to collect a large amount of evidence before making a decision.** As soon as the best option becomes clear, take it. Do not keep looking for further evidence to support what you feel is the right path to take.
● **deciding in an instant and then analysing and doubting the decision after the event.** Sometimes snap decisions are needed. Don't keep going back over things you are no longer able to change.
● **passing the buck.** Too often, people say they need their boss to endorse a decision when actually they don't. Be confident in your own judgement.
● **constantly falling into the same trap.** Over time, you'll get a sense of where you tend to make good decisions and where you make the wrong choice. Learn from your decisions to improve future performance.

Things to do

You'll be more decisive and probably make more good decisions if you try to:

● **listen to your instinct.** Then use the facts to support what feels like the right thing to do or challenge what doesn't.

- **make the decision that benefits most people.** Don't just make the one that simply benefits you.
- **think before following the herd.** Before doing the same action as everyone else, reflect on it and, if you believe it's wrong, prove it by going against the tide.
- **take responsibility for your decisions.** Be prepared to take ownership of them even if they prove with time not to have been the best ones.

 Sometimes others will give you plenty of reasons to make a decision they themselves are reluctant to make. If you're going to take the lead, clear your desk of their arguments and base your decision on your own research.

Avoid procrastination

This is one of the biggest challenges we all face. Many of us find it hard to take decisive action over important or difficult tasks, and we put off the jobs we really don't feel like doing. The trouble is, if you always do the jobs that appeal most first, you might lack sufficient time and energy to for the more challenging things you've been putting off.

Procrastination becomes a habit. In fact, in some organizations, people have learned that, if you put something off for long enough, it will eventually become unnecessary. It's rather like a small boy refusing to brush his teeth after a meal. If he can put off the task successfully until bedtime, he might not have to brush them at all.

At work, putting things off because you don't want to do them can be dangerous if the unpopular task relates to health and safety, for example routine equipment maintenance. Alternatively, if people get away without doing something, then perhaps it no longer needs to be done. Sometimes work practices don't adapt quickly enough when new processes or technology make them redundant.

To avoid procrastination:

- schedule into your work the tasks you might otherwise avoid
- don't say you'll wait for the right moment; it might never come
- set aside time for potential distractions such as email and keep your quality work time as just that.

Case study

Charity worked as an administrator at a care home. She loved making sure that everything ran smoothly. She particularly liked organizing visits by people like the chiropodist and physiotherapist. She also enjoyed organizing the shift rotas so that the home was always fully staffed.

What Charity did not like doing was the bookkeeping. She convinced herself that it was far more important to make sure that the needs of the residents were met than those of the group accountant at head office. Invoices were often late going out and the home's cash flow began to suffer.

When the home manager suggested a 'finance for non-financial managers' course to Charity, she agreed. She had now realized how important it was to make her work on the accounts more of a priority.

Summary

Today we've identified the difference that being paid for your time makes to the way you manage that time. It's still your time, but at work you've committed to exchange it for money. We've seen how this means that you have to accept tasks, deadlines and objectives you might not choose for yourself.

That said, you're not going to be a pushover. A brief introduction to the concept of transactional analysis highlighted the importance of maintaining an adult relationship with your boss. Without it you increase your risk of being bossed around and losing control of your workload.

Lastly, we looked at the problems that await you if you become indecisive and put things off. You are now more aware of the dangers of procrastination. You perhaps can now remember instances where, by putting something off, it became far harder to do than if you had dealt with it earlier.

SUNDAY

MONDAY

TUESDAY

WEDNESDAY

THURSDAY

FRIDAY

SATURDAY

Fact-check (answers at the back)

1. Why does time management matter more at work than at home?
   a) You spend more waking hours at work than home ❏
   b) At work your employer is buying your time from you ❏
   c) Your boss gives you too much to do and at home you like being lazy ❏
   d) It doesn't ❏

2. Unless managed properly, what can your work time do?
   a) Spill over into your private life ❏
   b) Become very boring ❏
   c) Catch you by surprise when it's time to go home so soon ❏
   d) Become dangerous ❏

3. What can our natural desire to please lead us to do?
   a) Waste time with small talk ❏
   b) Buy cakes for everyone every day ❏
   c) Overcommit ❏
   d) Be seen as a soft touch ❏

4. What is likely to happen if you respond to your manager in an emotional, childlike way?
   a) Your manager will become bossier, like a parent ❏
   b) You will lose the respect of your peers ❏
   c) They might give you a tissue to dry your eyes ❏
   d) You'll soon both find yourselves playing games ❏

5. If there are things your boss does really badly, what should you do?
   a) Show them up by telling their boss ❏
   b) Set her or him up to fail at every opportunity ❏
   c) Tell them to go on a course ❏
   d) Compensate for the weak area by doing more yourself ❏

6. What happens when you procrastinate?
   a) You get things done quickly ❏
   b) You put off making decisions ❏
   c) You delegate things you don't like to others ❏
   d) You think too long about things before deciding what to do ❏

7. What will happen if you insist on getting your manager to check every decision you make?
   a) They will respect your commitment to include them ❏
   b) You will be likely to get put forward for promotion ❏
   c) You will be even more highly valued ❏
   d) Neither you nor your manager will get as much done ❏

8. To whom or what should you pay attention when making a decision?
   a) Your instinct ❏
   b) Your mum ❏
   c) Your boss ❏
   d) A counsellor ❏

9. If time proves you to have made a poor decision, what should you do?

a) Dwell on it and make yourself feel bad ☐

b) Stop making decisions until you work out how to get it right every time ☐

c) Accept it and move on, knowing that on the day it seemed right ☐

d) Make sure you ask all your colleagues for their opinion next time ☐

10. Emails are perhaps the biggest distraction in any office. What's the best way to deal with them?

a) Answer them the moment they come in ☐

b) Wait until you've got a certain number and then deal with them ☐

c) Auto-forward them to someone else to deal with ☐

d) Set aside specific times throughout the day and deal with them then ☐

SUNDAY
MONDAY
TUESDAY
WEDNESDAY
THURSDAY
FRIDAY
SATURDAY

TUESDAY

Organizing your workspace

So far we've looked at how you can develop a clear personal vision for your future, which will help you become more focused and make it easier for you to manage your time effectively. We also explored your job and your relationship with your boss, and how to manage the balance of power so that you can influence the work you are given.

Now it's time to focus on some practical ways in which you can work more efficiently. Today we'll take a look at your workspace. You might have your own office or a desk in an open-plan space. You might even have a workshop or work at home. What we'll cover today is applicable to all these situations.

Today we look at the most basic time management techniques. You'll have heard many of the tips before, but this time we'll try to cover them in ways that are easy to follow. I want you to know how things could be done but I also want to show you how to do them differently.

By the end of today you will have:

- a tidier desk
- simplified your computer desktop
- done some filing and filled the bin.

Your desk

I spend most of my working life at my desk. You probably do the same. It's the place where I put things when I come in from a meeting. It's where I put the day's post when it arrives and where I use my computer. A lot of stuff arrives on my desk. Less of it leaves.

When I look up from my screen, I look out through a glass wall at trees, fields and in the distance, a few houses. I'm lucky to have such a nice view from my desk. I enjoy watching the seasons change, the clouds, vapour trails from passing planes and the cats that play outside my window. It's a wonder I get any work done at all!

'I like work, it fascinates me. I can sit and look at it for hours.'

Jerome K. Jerome

Your field of vision

As you read this page, the centres of your eyes are focused on the line of text. You can see it clearly. However, as I prompt you to notice it, you will become aware of your peripheral vision. You are now aware of objects and movement on either side of the book (or screen) you are reading. If you are reading on a train, you will notice when the person sitting next to you scratches their nose or turns the page of their book or newspaper.

Your peripheral vision is constantly scanning the space around you and alerting your brain to what it detects. It's a defence mechanism because our eyes face forwards, making us vulnerable to prey approaching from the side. It also means that all the clutter on your desk is also literally on your mind. You cannot shut out the distraction, so you have to remove it.

It's simple to improve your view.

● **Put nice things within your field of vision.**
I have flowers, sea shells, a stone from the beach and, when it's late, a scented candle.

● **Remove nasty things from your desk.**
If something annoys you, deal with it or file it away until you can deal with it. In view it will nag at your mind.

● **Keep your desk, keyboard and screen nice and clean.**
Get rid of those coffee stains, bits of Blu-tack™ and crumbs from your lunch.

Case study

Jonathan has had a lifelong fascination with helicopters. He hopes to learn to fly one before he is 35 and own one before he is 40. On his desk, just to the left of his computer screen, is a model helicopter. It reminds him throughout the working day of his ambition.

What's on your desk?

What do you actually need on your desk? In truth you need very little, yet we almost all have untidy desks. The reason is often procrastination: we leave things on our desks because we have yet to decide what to do with them. They are too important to throw out and too complex to deal with immediately.

Here's how to clear your desk:

1 Start at one side and work across. Pick everything up and put it in one of three places:
   - the bin – because it's not important
   - a file, ideally in a cabinet so you can close the drawer and hide it
   - back on your desk because it is work in progress.
2 Now take a closer look at what you've got left because you're not sure what to do with it:
   - business cards – we all collect them, but add the details to your email address book and you can throw them away. Sync your address book with your mobile
   - work in progress – go through the papers and bin what's no longer relevant. Do not print out copies of emails or other documents unless you are constantly referring to them; your computer already has the information
   - your computer and printer – put the main tower on the floor and the printer on another table, anywhere but your desk. Get longer leads so that all you have on your desk is keyboard, mouse and screen
   - Post-it™ notes – keep these handy but only if you promise not to stick notes to yourself around your screen. That will only distract you
   - 'homeless' papers – these are the things people have passed to you in case you need them, or you have printed out to read later, but not got round to yet. As a rule of thumb, if these have not been touched in a week, you can throw them out.

Many time management books recommend that you have an in-tray and make sure it's empty at the end of each day. I prefer an in-pile on the corner of the desk. That's because, if it gets too high, it will slip off on to the floor, reminding you to stop hoarding!

Your computer

Many people use a laptop at the office so that they can take it away with them and work from home and elsewhere. Smartphones and tablets are even easier to carry and enable you to keep in touch on the move. If you use a laptop or tablet, invest in a docking system so that you can still use a full-sized keyboard, mouse and screen.

Use two screens

My own efficiency leapt as soon as I started using two screens. Most computers can support two monitors and those that can't need very little adaptation. Using two screens means you can:

- view two applications at once
- easily cut and paste words, images and figures to and from documents
- keep working while an application is loading
- video conference using Skype while viewing the documents you're discussing at the same time.

This might seem like an invitation to become distracted, but actually it works really well. Here's how I use my two screens. I use my left-hand screen for things I want to look at and my right-hand screen for things I'm going to write. This also means that, whenever I cut and paste, it's from the left-hand screen to the right.

Left-hand screen	Right-hand screen
• Google	• Email
• Excel	• Word
• Skype	
• Viewing PDFs	

Organize your computer desktop

There are many ways to organize your computer desktop. It might be that your organization has an intranet and its own systems and applications. Or you might simply use the usual Microsoft applications or their freeware rivals. Whichever applies to you, there are some quick and easy ways to manage your computer desktop.

- **Keep it clear** – file or delete stray files and keep your desktop blank.
- **Start it easily** – add the things you use regularly to your Start menu in the bottom left-hand corner of your screen. This will save time.
- **Set your Internet browser** to open with your most commonly used tabs. Mine, for example, opens with my Google homepage, my Google Calendar and Twitter.

Additionally, my Google homepage has been set up to show me a number of newsfeeds and alerts. This means I can easily keep an eye on what's happening in my work world at a glance. Then I don't feel the need to surf and search unless it's for something I'm specifically researching.

TIP *Always make sure your PC backs up regularly and that you know how to retrieve your back-up if your PC fails or your laptop is stolen. No amount of good time management can compensate for the needless loss of your work.*

Make your computer faster

You are probably not a computer expert. If you work in a large organization, there'll be someone who maintains your PC for you. But that doesn't mean it's not helpful to know the questions to ask to make sure your PC is as fast and efficient as possible.

Here are some useful tips.

- **Do a weekly clean-up.**
  Use a specialist program to clear out all that digital clutter. Computers pick up lots of 'temporary' files and others bits and bobs. A weekly purge will stop them building up and slowing you down.

- **Check security settings.**
  Be realistic about security. Anti-virus software can slow your machine down but is essential. Beware over-zealous spam filtering and password protecting files. This will hit your efficiency too.

- **Make history history.**
  Set your web browser to keep only your recent history. A bursting web history will slow your browser down, so bookmark things you want to go back to.

Use voice recognition and commands

There are some really useful voice recognition packages available now. These will learn the way you speak and even remember the way you most usually use words. This makes them remarkably accurate. If your keyboard speed is slow, dictating to your PC will be considerably faster.

When using voice recognition software, pause after each paragraph to check and edit what's been written. This will stop you rambling and keep your writing tight. It also makes it far less likely for word errors to slip through to your final document.

SUNDAY MONDAY TUESDAY WEDNESDAY THURSDAY FRIDAY SATURDAY

Your filing

How often do you look at all the pictures you took on your last holiday? Digital cameras make it really easy to take plenty of photos but, if you're like me, you'll rarely make the time to go back and look at them later.

Your work files may be much the same. We all like to keep stuff and it's an easy thing to do. But perhaps less than 10 per cent of it is ever needed or looked at again. We keep stuff because we've always kept stuff.

Filing or archiving?

Filing is not the same as archiving. Archiving is retaining documents you don't need but must keep. In many business sectors, some documents and files need to be retained for as long as seven years. This may be a legal requirement or, if the work you're doing is publicly funded, a condition of contract. This is so that all of the detail can be audited if necessary.

Filing...

- is for documents you need again
- needs to be convenient for your desk.

Archiving...

- is for documents others may need again
- needs to be well away from your desk.

44

How to file

In your filing cabinet as well as on your computer, files need to be arranged in a logical and sensible way. Only those that relate to your current project load need to be near and handy. If, for example, you have a three-drawer filing cabinet, you could label the drawers (from the top) as follows.

Current projects	Proposed projects	Recent projects
• One folder for each • Filed alphabetically.	• One folder for each project you are likely to work on soon • Filed with the soonest at the front.	• Thinned-out folders of projects as you complete them • Filed with the newest at the front.

Unless you are obliged to retain files for a certain period, keep only a fixed number of recent projects on file. Each time you add a new file to the drawer, remove and throw away the oldest one.

Files are best kept in card wallets, with the contents in date order and all the same way up. If you are left-handed, you will want to file papers the opposite way up from right-handed people.

What to file

A filing system is like a vegetable plot: unless you keep on top of the weeding, the success you are cultivating will become choked and lost. The simple fact is that if you keep too much paperwork, it will become increasingly difficult to find the important documents you do need.

As a rule of thumb:

Keep	Do not keep
• Contracts • Important letters • Meeting notes (always date them)	• Draft contracts • Routine letters • Printed copies of emails • Anything you have on your computer

File management

Every time I take out a file I flick through it. This enables me to:

- quickly remind myself what I'm keeping, and why
- pull out and bin documents I no longer need.

> **TIP** *Always label the hanging files in which you keep your papers. Then if you cannot find the file card wallet when you want to add a document, you have somewhere to put it. This avoids the danger of creating a new second file for the same project.*

The paperless office

People have long talked about the paperless office. Originally the idea was that documents would be scanned when they arrived and the originals destroyed (or archived). Few made it work successfully.

Today, however, it is far easier to operate a paperless office. Indeed, some people dispense with an office altogether and work wherever they happen to be. The paperless office is easier to achieve than ever before because:

- 'cloud computing', or web-based personal filing systems, enable you to recover documents and information anywhere you have Internet access
- smartphones and tablet computers are giving us permanent Internet access wherever we go
- online file sharing means you can create a virtual office and limit access to documents to those you want to share them with.

Summary

Today we've looked at where you work and how you organize the space around you. We've looked at your physical space and your virtual space, both in your computer and online.

You were reminded of the importance of removing distracting clutter from your field of vision, and then encouraged to fill in some of that space with things that make you feel good and make you happy. Even if you don't sit near a window, you can bring the outdoors into your office.

I made a plea for you to consider using two screens with your computer. This might mean asking your boss to spend some money, but my experience says that the investment will be quickly recouped in increased efficiency. We also looked at how to simplify access to the programs and content you use the most. Use your common sense and a little time to get your own computer in order.

Lastly we talked about paper. We all keep too much of it for far too long. You now have some tips and techniques to take you closer to a paperless office. This is something we will all achieve one day.

SUNDAY
MONDAY
TUESDAY
WEDNESDAY
THURSDAY
FRIDAY
SATURDAY

Fact-check (answers at the back)

1. At your desk, why is it good to keep your field of vision uncluttered?
   a) Because even stuff you can only see peripherally will distract you ❑
   b) Because you'll lose things if you leave them on your desk ❑
   c) Because your boss will think you're more organized if you have a tidy desk ❑
   d) Because people will borrow things if you leave them lying around ❑

2. What's a good thing to have close to your computer where you can easily see it?
   a) A list of all the jobs you haven't got round to yet ❑
   b) An object that reminds you of a life ambition or goal ❑
   c) Your lunch ❑
   d) Your wallet or bag ❑

3. What should you do with a document that has been lying on your desk unread for a week?
   a) File it away with other papers you'll read when you have time ❑
   b) Throw it away ❑
   c) Give it to someone else to worry about ❑
   d) Hide it where it can't distract you ❑

4. What will using two screens on your desk do?
   a) Make you look important ❑
   b) Make you feel important ❑
   c) Make you more efficient ❑
   d) Confuse you ❑

5. What should your computer desktop screen have on it?
   a) All your current project files ❑
   b) Holiday photos ❑
   c) Webcam images so you can see what's happening at home ❑
   d) As little as possible ❑

6. How can you make your computer work more efficiently and swiftly?
   a) Download some clever freeware when nobody's looking ❑
   b) Avoid spilling coffee on the keyboard ❑
   c) Get rid of temporary files and other junk at least weekly ❑
   d) Don't turn if off at night ❑

7. Where should you keep archived files?
   a) Close to your desk ❑
   b) In a bank of filing cabinets along the office wall ❑
   c) Where you can get at them but nowhere near where you work ❑
   d) With all your other files ❑

8. If you can't find the right file for the document you need to put away, what should you do?
   a) Keep it where the file should be ❑
   b) Create a second file ❑
   c) Search the place for the missing file ❑
   d) Throw it away ❑

9. What do cloud computing and tablet technology mean for tomorrow's office?
a) It will be just as cluttered as today's ❏
b) It will be almost entirely paperless ❏
c) It will be full of screens and computers ❏
d) It will be full of plants and flowers ❏

10. What will you have if you do even half the things suggested today?
a) A better-organized workspace ❏
b) A headache ❏
c) The envy of your colleagues ❏
d) No need to read any more of this book ❏

SUNDAY

MONDAY

TUESDAY

WEDNESDAY

THURSDAY

FRIDAY

SATURDAY

WEDNESDAY

Managing your workload

Now that you are almost halfway through this book, you will have already improved your time management. Your tidy desk and the beginnings of a filing system are outward signs of the progress you're making. Others will be starting to notice.

But work keeps piling up. Even though you're more confidently challenging the assumption that you'll do whatever you're asked, stuff keeps coming your way. Today we'll look in detail at how you manage your time. We'll strike at the very heart of your time management issues and make it easier to cope with the flow.

Today we'll focus on practical techniques, putting into action many of the principles I've already introduced to you. Much of what we cover is little more than common sense. That's because, at times, we all need encouragement to step back from our day-to-day routine and see what would be obvious if we weren't so busy.

When you finish this chapter, you will have:

- discovered how to manage the size of your workload
- become more proficient at scheduling your time
- developed your own way of prioritizing tasks.

Your workload

Cyril Northcote Parkinson described perfectly a phenomenon you probably recognize only too well. He said that 'Work expands so as to fill the time available for its completion.' People call this 'Parkinson's Law'. In practical terms this means that, however much or little people have to do, they always seem busy. The solution to managing your workload is therefore not to work harder but to work smarter.

'Choose a job you love, and you will never have to work a day in your life.'

Confucius

Work SMART

SMART is an acronym that stands for Specific, Measurable, Achievable, Relevant and Timed. The more you define your workload in SMART terms, the easier it will be to define and manage.

Let's take this book as an example. If my editor had simply said, 'Go and write a book on time management', I would have struggled with the task. Who is the book aimed at? How complicated or detailed must it be? When is it needed and where will it fit in the marketplace? We actually agreed some

SMART objectives. These enabled me to work efficiently and effectively. It also means that my editor will get the book he commissioned, not something completely different. Here's what we agreed:

● **Specific**
I would write a practical guide to time management for people who probably work in an office.

● **Measurable**
The book would be less than 25,000 words with a structure common to all books in the series.

● **Achievable**
We both knew I could do it, not because I am a time management guru, but because I can relate to the subject and recognize the need.

● **Relevant**
The current economic climate means we all have to work harder. Good time management is thus really important.

● **Timed**
I had a deadline by which the book had to be submitted. It's no coincidence that that was also the day I finished writing it!

I therefore knew precisely what was expected of me. Had this not been the case, I could have spent months researching the subject in too much detail. I could also have produced a far larger book that you'd have found too expensive and left on the shelf. By sticking to agreed SMART objectives life's been easier and the book more successful.

When you agree to accept any project, make sure you agree SMART objectives. Then and only then can you schedule the task and be confident you'll deliver what's expected.

When your manager gives you a task, discuss with her or him the SMART objectives. This will encourage her or him to think in SMART terms too.

Schedule your work

We have already looked at the value of splitting your day into quarters. For most of us that means dividing it into two-hour chunks. Now that you are starting to view your work in SMART terms, you can see that there's potential to plot your workload in far more detail.

Many organizations use specialist project management software to schedule complex projects. This produces what is effectively a diary upon which tasks are mapped. By breaking the project down into tasks, each with an expected duration and deadline for completion, you can construct a matrix that shows what needs to be done when. This is called a Gantt chart and enables a project manager to share out tasks and coordinate their delivery efficiently.

You can do the same thing using your diary. If you use an online diary, you can link it to a task list. Each task needs to be relatively short, so that you don't simply set aside a whole day to work on 'the project'. By breaking a project into tasks, you will know whether you are on schedule.

I scheduled my work in this way when writing this book. I set aside time to do the research, then time to write it. I also allowed time to plan what would be on each page of the book, so that the finished work covered everything I wanted to share. Finally, knowing how quickly I write and the need for breaks,

I blocked out days for writing in my diary. Only then did I know when to start and when I would finish.

Don't schedule all of your time. Allow half a day a week for general admin and always give yourself time for slippage. If you schedule every minute of your day, there is a danger of feeling trapped by your workload. Be efficient, but accept that you are human too!

The 80:20 rule

This is also called the Pareto Principle. In 1906 Vilfredo Pareto noticed that 80 per cent of the land in his native Italy was owned by 20 per cent of the people. Research showed him that this was also true elsewhere. Later, people began to see that the 80:20 rule applies to almost any situation. For example:

- 80 per cent of profits come from 20 per cent of your customers
- 80 per cent of the time you wear clothes from 20 per cent of your wardrobe
- 80 per cent of photocopier breakdowns are caused by 20 per cent of the users.

More relevant to how you spend your time is the fact that probably just 20 per cent of your time produces 80 per cent of the results. Conversely, 80 per cent of your time therefore delivers just 20 per cent of your work output.

Set priorities

To make the best use of your time, you need to spend as much of it as possible on the most valuable projects. These will be those that:

- deliver the most financial return to your organization
- are of the greatest strategic importance
- take you closer to your own personal and career ambitions.

In a large organization, where perhaps you feel like a small cog in a very large wheel, setting priorities can be difficult. You may not always know the full significance of the task you've been asked urgently to complete. That's why good managers will explain the bigger picture.

TIP *If managers tell their people why something is important, it will become more important to their people.*

It will help you set priorities if you sort your work into one of these four categories.

1 Very urgent Very important	3 Less urgent Very important
2 Very urgent Less important	4 Less urgent Less important

It's obvious that you need to complete the tasks you've placed in box 1 first. You might label these red, so you know they are both the most important and the most urgent.

Next you have to decide between tasks in boxes 2 and 3. You might label these blue and green. In the abstract, deciding if urgency or importance is more significant is impossible. In reality, when you are looking at real tasks, the choices become much easier. That's because few tasks or projects occur in complete isolation – they all form part of a perpetual flow of activity.

As you schedule your time, you will clearly focus on those from box 1, marked red. Then you will fill in your time with those from boxes 2 and 3, blue and green. So now you should be eager to push away anything that is not important or urgent.

Deal with 'stuff'

You might think that you can ignore the less urgent, less important tasks altogether, but unfortunately this is rarely the case. Yes, some can be dumped in the bin and others delegated, but many will still need your attention eventually. For one thing, they might not be urgent or important now but they may become so with time, as with the following examples.

● Updating policy and procedure documents might not seem important or urgent until an audit or inspection finds you are no longer compliant with legislation or, worse, are in breach of a contract.

- Routine equipment maintenance can be put off when you are busy with important and urgent tasks, but leave it too long and a breakdown will play havoc with your scheduling.
- Requests for information from students doing project work can be ignored. But what if your organization wants to recruit talented graduates? Might some of these be the very young people you are ignoring right now?

There will be days when you are not in the mood for intense, challenging tasks, perhaps because you feel tired or under the weather. These moments are an ideal time for setting aside half a day to clear a backlog of odd jobs, as a break from more demanding tasks.

Always make time for 'stuff' and keep on top of it.

> **'I recommend you take care of the minutes, and the hours will take care of themselves.'**
>
> Philip Stanhope, 4th Earl of Chesterfield

Free up more time

Author and lateral thinker Edward de Bono said, 'The brain's ability to set up routines is its most important function. Life would be impossible without routines. To go through all the ways of getting dressed with eleven items of clothing could take years, as there are 39,916,800 ways of getting dressed. Like trains on railway tracks, our thoughts and feelings are predetermined paths.'

I guess you did not take years to get dressed this morning. It's also probably true that many of the routine tasks of your daily life are conducted as if by clockwork, following an established routine. For example, I always read the sections of the Sunday newspaper in the same sequence. You too will have routines you follow without thinking.

We also create routines at work. The tasks we habitually need to do are usually done without much thought at all. However, circumstances change and the need for those routine tasks changes also. But habit means that we carry on as before.

SUNDAY
MONDAY
TUESDAY
WEDNESDAY
THURSDAY
FRIDAY
SATURDAY

Case study

Every Saturday morning I would visit the office building I own and empty the tenants' wastepaper baskets. The cleaner did this on Tuesdays and Thursdays, so my weekly round with a bin bag neatly filled the gap.

Then the cleaner's routine changed so that she visited on Wednesday and Sunday. It was only when she commented on how tidy the place was on Sundays that I realized I no longer needed to empty the bins on Saturday. The task had become a fixed part of my Saturday routine, so that, even though I knew the cleaner had changed her days, it had not occurred to me to stop emptying the bins on Saturday.

In business, habitual behaviour can reduce the cost saving of investment and innovation. A new machine in a factory might mean that an earlier process is no longer required. Often, though, that process will continue, quite simply because it always has.

Are you doing things by habit? Think about everything you do in a typical day and make a list of the things you probably don't or no longer need to do.

Summary

Today we've looked at managing your workload by working SMART. Agreeing and using SMART project and task objectives is perhaps the best way to manage expectations. If your manager or customer expected more – or less – whatever you've actually done will not be appreciated. Working SMART will make life easier: you will not go on beyond the point at which you did as much as was expected, and you can more accurately schedule your work.

We also looked at prioritizing so that you include in your work programme the most important, most urgent tasks first. We then justified the need to make time for all the assorted 'stuff' that inevitably needs doing, even though it's not particularly urgent or important.

Lastly, we reflected on the idea of habits. Habits create activity shortcuts, so that you can complete routine tasks quickly and effectively in the same sequence each time. However, the danger of habits is that you'll continue them after they cease to be necessary. We need to think about changing them, to avoid situations that are like walking to the local school every afternoon even though your child has grown up and gone to university.

SUNDAY
MONDAY
TUESDAY
WEDNESDAY
THURSDAY
FRIDAY
SATURDAY

Fact-check (answers at the back)

1. What does Parkinson's Law say?
   a) The more work you have, the more time you will find ☐
   b) Work expands to fill the time available for its completion ☐
   c) Time expands to accommodate the work you have to do ☐
   d) However little work you have, you will always find plenty to do ☐

2. What does the S in the acronym SMART stand for?
   a) Specific ☐
   b) Successful ☐
   c) Simple ☐
   d) Sensible ☐

3. What does the M in the acronym SMART stand for?
   a) Measurable ☐
   b) Marvellous ☐
   c) Meaningful ☐
   d) Me ☐

4. What does the A in the acronym SMART stand for?
   a) Accessible ☐
   b) Available ☐
   c) Achievable ☐
   d) Anywhere ☐

5. What does the R in the acronym SMART stand for?
   a) Rational ☐
   b) Replicable ☐
   c) Responsible ☐
   d) Realistic ☐

6. What does the T in the acronym SMART stand for?
   a) Troublesome ☐
   b) Timely ☐
   c) Timed ☐
   d) Tense ☐

7. What does the Pareto Principle state?
   a) 80 per cent of the activity delivers 20 per cent of the result ☐
   b) 20 per cent of the activity delivers 80 per cent of the result ☐
   c) 80 per cent of the time is wasted and 20 per cent is not ☐
   d) 20 per cent of my work achieves as much as 80 per cent of yours ☐

8. When setting priorities, what will be the most important tasks?
   a) Those that are very urgent and very important ☐
   b) Those that are less urgent and less important ☐
   c) Those that are very urgent and less important ☐
   d) Those that are less urgent and very important ☐

9. When is the best time to deal with unimportant stuff that isn't urgent?
   a) When you're at your very best and can conquer anything ☐
   b) When you need a break and it won't be too taxing to do ☐
   c) When you're off sick and feel the need to do some work ☐
   d) When someone's shouting because suddenly it's become more urgent ☐

10. Why is it good periodically to challenge the tasks we do through habit?

a) Otherwise we might take them for granted ❑

b) We want to do them really well ❑

c) We might forget how to do them if we don't think now and then ❑

d) They may no longer be important ❑

SUNDAY

MONDAY

TUESDAY

WEDNESDAY

THURSDAY

FRIDAY

SATURDAY

THURSDAY

Coping with your colleagues

None of us works in complete isolation; we all have to rely on other people to help us achieve our work goals. But other people can also hinder our efforts to manage time effectively. We need to strike a happy balance. Too serious and work-focused and people won't want to help you. Too playful and easily distracted and you'll get nothing done. It's something we all have to cope with.

Today we're going to explore how you can work more effectively with your colleagues. You will learn some useful techniques that will help you better manage your interactions with others. We all need each other if we are to succeed, so don't be selfish and overlook the needs of your colleagues. They may need your help to see the benefits to them of managing time better.

As you read through this section, try out the tips and techniques. Not all will be relevant and some will be tougher to do than others. By the end of today you will be better able to:

- manage delegation, both ways
- avoid distraction
- make meetings more effective.

Make delegation work for you

A good way to get more done is to get other people to help you. If you line manage others, they will expect you to delegate work to them. But you also need to delegate to colleagues, both within your team and often across the wider organization. At times you may also need to delegate to your manager.

'We wander for distraction, but we travel for fulfilment.'

Hilaire Belloc

Earn the respect of others

People will do more for you if they want to help you. Even if you're someone's boss, you'll get more done if they respect you than if you simply issue orders. Here are some ways you can make it easier for others to respect you at work.

● **Respect yourself.**
Self-respect is not a given; we all doubt ourselves from time to time. Self-criticism and doubt can be harmful. It's difficult to respect someone who doesn't respect themselves.

● **Respect others.**
Being respectful to others will encourage others to respect you in return. Respect their views, priorities and prejudices even if they differ from your own. You don't have to agree with people in order to respect them.

● **Be realistic.**
Don't expect too much of yourself or those you delegate to. Don't lose perspective or objectivity. Agree what is to be done and by when.

● **Be selective.**
Distance yourself from bullies and other toxic people. If you let others push you around, you'll be tempted to do the same yourself.

Case study

Margaret had recently been promoted to team leader in a busy call centre. She found it tough being boss, although she enjoyed the responsibility of this bigger role. What really troubled her was that she was now managing people she had worked alongside for years.

Her parents had instilled a strict work ethic in Margaret from an early age. This made her a little too quick to be critical when her new team seemed less focused than she would be herself. She picked up that people were calling her 'Bossy Margaret' and was upset that people were misjudging her in this way. All she wanted was to improve performance.

Her own manager suggested she see a counsellor. Within a few weeks Margaret realized she was pushing her people in the same way her mother had pushed her. With the counsellor's help, she came to see how this wasn't helping her win the respect of her team. Soon her relationship with her team improved.

TIP People have short memories. If you change, others will respond to the way you are now and forget how you were before.

Rules for delegation

If someone reports to you and you are delegating them tasks, there are some basic rules that will help you.

1 Right person
Make sure you ask someone with the skills and knowledge to do the job.

2 Right task
Explain clearly what you want done, why and by when.

3 Right resources
Ensure that whatever's needed to do the job is available. This applies as much to information as equipment.

4 Right support
Make sure people know how to get help if they encounter a problem or need more resources. If you are the support, how will they contact you?

5 Right reward
Unless people can see what's in it for them, the tasks you delegate will feel like a burden.

If you are delegating to someone who does not report to you, explaining 'what's in it for them' is even more important. You have to 'sell, not tell'.

Deal with distractions

We all get distracted from time to time. Your susceptibility to distraction will to some extent depend on your personality. Some of us are far more easily distracted than others! Let's look at some of the things that can distract you and how you can minimize their impact.

Time thieves

These are people who seem to have nothing more important to do than stop you working. They are the workplace equivalent of those irritating neighbours who seem to wait and pounce on you the moment you go out of your door. They are often lonely and simply want to chat.

You find this at work too, where time thieves will appear in a number of guises.

- **Negative people** want you to support their latest complaint. Say that while you sympathize, you're busy right now and can't spare the time.
- **Gloomy people** want to explain why in their view what you're doing is not going to work out. Tell them you have to find out for yourself and please can they let you get on.
- **Adoring people** see you as successful and think that, by hanging round you, some of your success will rub off on them. Encourage them to earn your patronage by doing something useful to help.
- **Lost people** have taken on more than they can really handle and now want you to help them with their work. These are difficult to shift if you feel sorry for them. Be firm, point them in the right direction and let them go.

Social media

After email, which we'll talk about tomorrow, social media are perhaps the biggest distraction in most offices today. In small organizations in particular, websites such as Facebook, Twitter and to a lesser extent LinkedIn are becoming massive distractions. You only have to look at fellow commuters on the train, bus or even on foot to see the extent of the problem. Everyone spends their travelling time online, updating their Facebook and Tweeting their thoughts.

Twitter, in particular, is now widely used in the workplace to research, market and recruit. Journalists, for example, are often most easily contacted via Twitter. You can also use Twitter to follow proceedings at conferences and events, and even to monitor what rival organizations are saying and doing.

As with other business tools, social media websites need to be used sensibly and at specific times. For some of us, me included, the temptation to monitor debate and comment on Twitter about often highly relevant topics is almost overwhelming. The simple fact is, however, that you can't be part of every conversation, read every article or comment on every debate.

The best way to use social media at work is to:

- be very focused about what you want it to help you achieve
- set aside a number of 10- or 15-minute slots each day to use it
- use these slots as breaks between larger tasks, coffee breaks even
- take the trouble to learn how to use it properly so your time spent on these websites is more productive.

Other distractions

Many other things can distract you during the working day. Here are some of them, together with suggested ways of reducing their impact.

- **Yourself**
  If you have ideas for projects other than the one on your desk right now, keep a notebook and jot down a reminder. Go back to it later.

- **Passing traffic**
  If your desk is near the toilets or kitchen you may have lots of people passing by. Position yourself so they don't catch your attention as they pass.

- **Phone calls**
  Use voicemail or divert to a colleague when you need time to concentrate without distraction. There might be occasions when you have time to help colleagues by picking up their calls. Work together and help each other.

TIP *It's OK to say no. All you have to do is say it politely and give a reason.*

Make meetings more effective

Next time you go to a meeting, try to calculate how much it is costing. I don't mean for the room, coffee and biscuits, but for the people round the table. What is the salary bill for the afternoon likely to total? Your best guess is likely to produce a surprisingly high figure. Add the time taken to prepare, get there and return home again and you can see why it's so important to make meetings really effective.

Meetings are not all bad. When well managed and attended by the right people, they enable issues to be properly debated and good decisions made. Let's see how you can make sure the meetings you attend make best use of your time.

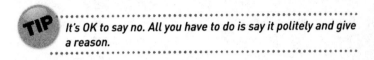

Why have meetings?

All meetings should have clear objectives. What are the decisions to be made? If the meeting is just to brief people, could this be done differently? The fact that you've always had a departmental meeting on the first Tuesday of the month is not sufficient reason to have one next month. Meetings, like so many other activities, become habit. Understand why you are meeting and state the objectives.

Who should come to the meeting?

If a meeting is to result in decisions being made, you need to have the right people round the table. If you can't get all the decision makers there, make sure they delegate authority to someone who can be there. Without the right people, a meeting can become pointless. Equally, don't assume that just because someone's always attended these meetings they still need to be there. Situations change and people may not always tell you they no longer need to attend.

TIP *If when you arrive for a meeting you are missing a key person or are not quorate, it's often better to stop and rearrange than to discuss things just because some of you are there.*

What's the meeting about?

The most important document in a meeting is the agenda. This should:

- list what is to be discussed, starting with the most important item and ending with the least important
- have start and end times for each item to keep things to time
- be supported where necessary by short, easy-to-read papers that explain the options. It is often also useful if the paper's author includes their recommendation
- have been circulated, with supporting papers, before the meeting so that people can prepare.

How should we run the meeting?

Good chairing is vital to a successful meeting. The chairperson should:

- check that people understand why they are there
- keep the meeting to time
- briefly set the scene for each agenda item
- invite, then chair, debate
- involve the quieter people who otherwise might not speak
- seek agreement or, if this is not possible, take a vote
- make sure someone reliable and unbiased records action points and, if necessary, full minutes.

Sometimes people get angry or confrontational in meetings. This can be disruptive, but at times it may also be vital if the real issues are to be discussed. Manage conflict sensitively. If the meeting degenerates, insist on a ten-minute break so that people can cool off. Encourage opponents to spend that time discussing their differences in private.

'Laughter drives shouting away.'
Indra Devi

Where shall we hold the meeting?

The best meetings take place where it's convenient for most of those attending. Technology means that far-flung participants can take part over the Internet, using teleconferencing or

Skype. It is possible to hold a meeting entirely online, either as voice only or using video too if you have sufficient bandwidth.

Meetings work best when held in a room that is:

- large enough for the number of people attending
- comfortable, neither too warm nor too cold and adequately lit and ventilated
- undisturbed by noise or other distraction
- available for as long as you need it.

Sometimes it can be useful to hold a meeting close to where the issues being discussed are most important. For example, if you're meeting about a factory extension, meet at the factory so you can see the site and get a feel for the context.

If your meeting ends ahead of time, it's not a problem, providing everyone has had the opportunity to contribute to the debate. Don't stretch a meeting out simply to fill the time set aside.

Case study

Michael ran a busy sales office. Every morning at nine he called the team together for a 15-minute daily briefing. The meeting took place in the main sales office with everyone standing in a large circle round the room.

Everyone was given the opportunity to say whether they:

- needed particular help with a job that day
- had good news to share from the day before
- had an idea to share that could improve sales performance.

Although up to 20 people sometimes attended the meeting, it always took no longer than 15 minutes. Michael's people all felt involved in what was going on.

Summary

Today we've seen that coping with people, particularly colleagues, is one of the toughest time management challenges. The paradox is that we need other people in order to succeed, but those who work with us can also be a distraction.

We saw the importance of delegation, and that it works well only when the person picking up your tasks clearly understands why the work needs doing and why it is to their advantage to do it punctually and well. It also helps if you have the respect of those you are delegating to.

In today's largely open-plan office environment, it's all too easy to get distracted. We looked at how you could minimize distractions, recognizing that some of us are more easily distracted than others.

Lastly, we talked about meetings, which need to be well organized and managed if they are not to become a costly waste of time and resources. You now have a better appreciation of what makes meetings useful. This will help you with any meeting you attend: you don't have to be chairing a meeting to influence its success.

SUNDAY

MONDAY

TUESDAY

WEDNESDAY

THURSDAY

FRIDAY

SATURDAY

Fact-check (answers at the back)

1. What is the first thing you need to do to win the respect of other people?
   a) Be nice to them ❑
   b) Pay them ❑
   c) Respect yourself ❑
   d) Respect them ❑

2. What does respecting someone else's point of view mean?
   a) Always agreeing with them ❑
   b) Trying to change their views to match your own ❑
   c) Sometimes agreeing to disagree ❑
   d) Getting frustrated when you cannot agree ❑

3. Before you delegate a task to someone, what should you make sure of first?
   a) That they have the knowledge and skills to do the job ❑
   b) You choose someone who won't give you a hard time ❑
   c) You're certain you don't have time to do it yourself ❑
   d) They have the time ❑

4. What should you always do when delegating a task to someone who doesn't report to you?
   a) Make sure their manager doesn't find out ❑
   b) Ask their manager's permission first ❑
   c) Make sure they can see how helping you will help them too ❑
   d) Pay them something, even if it's only lunch ❑

5. Why do time thieves steal your time?
   a) They don't know any better ❑
   b) They don't realize how busy you are ❑
   c) They are thick-skinned or just ignorant ❑
   d) You let them ❑

6. Your boss points out that you're spending too much time on Twitter. What do you say to her?
   a) She's wrong and it's worth every minute you spend there ❑
   b) She has a point and perhaps you need to schedule set times to use Twitter ❑
   c) It's none of her business how you spend your time as long as you do your job ❑
   d) You'll stop using Twitter during work time ❑

7. What should you do if you find there's less and less to discuss at your weekly departmental meetings?
   a) Create agenda items to make the meeting seem worth while ❑
   b) Suggest meeting only when there's enough to discuss ❑
   c) Invite people to offer new subjects they'd like to see discussed ❑
   d) Treat it as a training session and practise your debating skills ❑

8. What should you do if you're chairing a meeting and someone seems too shy to contribute?
a) Not bother to invite them next time ❏
b) Pick on them so they have to say something or look stupid ❏
c) Give them opportunities to comment without putting them on the spot ❏
d) Ignore them and concentrate on everyone else ❏

9. If your meeting is about a single issue about which not much is known, what should you do?
a) Only invite people already familiar with the issue ❏
b) Question the need to discuss it when you probably know the answer already ❏
c) Wait until you have more agenda items ❏
d) Organize a visit or at least a presentation so that people understand the context ❏

10. People are most likely to influence your time management if you are:
a) The boss ❏
b) Bottom of the pecking order ❏
c) Anywhere: we all need people to do our job ❏
d) In an open-plan office ❏

SUNDAY

MONDAY

TUESDAY

WEDNESDAY

THURSDAY

FRIDAY

SATURDAY

FRIDAY

Communicating effectively to save time

One thing that distinguishes us as a species is our communication. We never stop chattering to one another. You only have to go into a bar or restaurant to see the extent to which we all talk all the time. In fact, in a packed bar, we all talk more loudly, trying to be heard above the background noise.

Today we'll look at how you can improve your communication at work. The structured environment of the workplace means that you need to communicate in a more objective and precise way than you would in a social situation. At the same time you also need to remain friendly, because you need to have a good relationship with those working around you. No one wants to work with a surly grump who only speaks when absolutely necessary.

Increasingly, we are communicating online rather than speaking. It may seem more convenient to send an email than pick up the phone, but this can create problems, as it's easier to misinterpret written communication than it is when we simply talk to each other.

By the end of today you will have worked on your communication skills. In particular, you'll find yourself:

- speaking more meaningfully
- writing more clearly
- using email more efficiently.

Speaking

Talking to people is great. In a five-minute conversation you can raise an issue, discuss the options and agree an action. To do this by email would take a lot longer. Yet, too often, we persuade ourselves that email is more convenient than picking up the phone. That's not always the case.

Even something as simple as arranging an appointment with someone is so much faster when you pick up the phone and both open your diaries. So let's look at how, when and where you can use speech more effectively.

> *'Don't write anything you can phone. Don't phone anything you can talk.'*
>
> Earl Long

Face to face

If you're with someone, you can pick up on their body language as well as the words they use. This works in two ways, so the first thing you need to be aware of is that you'll get the decisions you want faster by looking as well as sounding committed. Our body language often conveys our meaning more accurately than our words. This also applies if you are video conferencing or using Skype, although to a lesser degree as cameras have a narrower field of vision than you.

Here are a few tips to help you get more from face-to-face conversation.

- Have a clear objective.
- Have answers to the most likely questions you'll be asked.
- Don't use words or jargon the other person might not understand.
- Listen to what the other person says.

Your 'elevator pitch'

If you meet someone really interesting by chance in an elevator, you've perhaps only got a minute to talk to them before the doors open and they step out. Always have your elevator pitch prepared and practised, so that when you meet someone new you can tell them in less than a minute who you are, what you do and why that might be of interest to them.

On the phone

The main difference between face-to-face conversation and a phone call is that you cannot see the person you are phoning. This sounds really obvious, but actually makes a big difference. Much of our communication is non-verbal, so when you only have voice you have to work harder to get the same result.

Here are some tips to help you achieve more from your phone calls.

- Start by asking if now is a good time; people answer the phone even when busy doing something else. Get their consent to continue the call.
- Get to the point. You can be more direct on the phone than face to face.
- Have paper and a pen beside the phone and note the key points.
- Summarize what you think has been agreed at the end of the call.
- Follow up in writing to confirm what happens next.

Here are some practical time-saving tips.

- Always leave a message if your call is answered by voicemail. Be sure to leave your name and suggest a good time for the person to call you back.
- Use speed dialling. If you make or receive a lot of calls, use software that identifies incoming numbers and opens the client record automatically.

Stand up when making important phone calls. It makes the call more focused and businesslike. This really works; try it!

Writing

For some reason, many people write differently from the way they speak. This is probably due to either a lack of confidence or a lack of practice. The only real difference between writing and speaking is that, when you write, you are not there to answer questions. This means that your writing has to be:

- **clear and easy to read**
  I always assume that English is not my readers' first language.
- **explicit**
  Get straight to the point and say it as you see it.
- **purposeful**
  Say what you want the reader to do next.

Short is sweet

The longer the message, the less likely people are to read and understand it. It is frequently true that the more words you need to use to get your message across, the less you've actually thought about what it is you are trying to say.

I hope, for example, that you find this book short and to the point. You could have spent a little more money and bought a time management book with twice as many pages. This would take longer to read and certainly not teach you twice as much.

Your memos, emails and letters will be quicker to write and faster to read if you:

- have a clear reason for writing before you start
- make no sentence more than 12 words long
- start with a summary, then go on to context, content and call to action.

Haiku

This Japanese form of poetry is beautifully simple and forces you to be concise. A Haiku has just three lines with a line pattern of five–seven–five syllables. For example:

Having been erased, (5)

The document you're seeking (7)

Must now be retyped. (5)

Try writing some of your business communication as simply as this!

Taking notes

We take notes to help us remember something. This works because:

- notes capture just the key points that are relevant to us
- the process of writing something down makes it easier to recall.

Make your notes:

- short and simple – what matters rather than all that was said
- personal to you – adding comments, underlines, stars or circles.

Consider creating mind maps. These diagrams enable your notes to build up along a number of strands, one for each theme you want to explore. Google 'mind mapping' to find out more.

Always have a notebook and pen, or even a phone with a notepad facility, in your bag or pocket. You can then jot things down when they occur to you.

Case study

Martin had quite a reputation as an after-dinner speaker. He enjoyed speaking, and was popular enough to charge a fee. His employer knew about his speaking and that he spoke only on Friday or Saturday nights.

What people really enjoyed were his humorous observations about everyday life. He always had new stories to tell. They were always very funny and, surprisingly, also true.

Martin always carried a notebook and would write down the strange things he saw people do or amusing phrases people used. From time to time he transferred his notes into a database so that he could find them again when researching a speech.

By day he was a management trainer and he used the same technique to fill his courses with laughter as well as learning.

Reading

When you first learned to read, your reading speed will have been quite slow. This is because you'll have looked at each and every word. New or unconfident readers also verbalize; they say what they are reading, even if internally.

Fluent readers, on the other hand, scan a line of text and read the shapes of the words, rather than looking at the individual letters that form each word. This is a form of speed-reading. The brain is familiar with word and phrase shapes and so helps your eyes out.

Imagine you have a long work document to read. You want to read it fast enough to get the meaning and slowly enough that you don't miss anything vital. You will read faster if you:

● run your finger slowly down the page and read just above it
● scan quickly but slow down as soon as a key word catches your eye
● highlight key words and sentences to go back to later
● finish the whole document before going back to just the highlighted areas.

> **TIP** *If you are reading on screen, use the 'find' function to take you straight to the words you are most interested in. For example, if you are in the insurance business, you might search for words like 'risk' or 'underwriting'.*

Emailing

Are you old enough to remember the days before email? It's hard for most of us to imagine how we'd operate without it now. Email enables us to communicate with many people round the world quickly and conveniently. It also enables us to send files that once would have had to be posted or taken by courier. Since we all spend increasing amounts of time reading, sending and replying to email, conquering our inbox is one of the most productive ways to improve our time management.

Managing emails

You can't stop people sending you emails, but you could probably manage them more efficiently. Here are some ways you can deal with incoming email.

- Turn off your email alert function so you are not distracted when an email comes in.
- Check emails every hour, not every minute.
- Create folders for each of your current projects.
- Create 'rules' so that emails are automatically filed by project.
- Use a spam filter to intercept unwanted email.
- Don't read emails copied to you unless they're clearly relevant to you.
- Resist the urge to reply straight away. Think first – do you need to reply?

Avoid the temptation to reply to an email simply to thank someone for sending you something you've been expecting. You don't need to be that polite with email.

Replying to emails

The subject line and sender should help you decide which emails to read first. You don't have to read them in the order they arrive. Here's what to do when you open an email.

1 If it's clearly not relevant to you, delete it.
2 Speed-read it to find what the writer expects of you.
3 Then do one of the following:
   - click reply and answer concisely
   - forward it to someone better able to deal with it
   - pop it in the relevant project folder if it contains information you will need again
   - delete it.
4 If the message is negative, it might be better answered by phone.

TIP *Do not keep thousands of emails on your computer. If they have to be kept, perhaps for legal reasons, organize a way of backing them up.*

Writing emails

Email is unique, and it benefits from being written in a style that is:

- more formal than if you are speaking face to face
- less formal than if you are writing a letter.

I think this applies even if you are emailing someone you've never met. You might not agree, in which case you need to do what works for you.

Remember, though, that one of the key benefits of email is the intimacy of the medium. Your unsolicited email will appear on the recipient's screen, perhaps sandwiched between emails from his or her colleagues.

When you write emails, try to:

- use the subject line to summarize the message in five or six words
- keep the email short, ideally less than 150 words
- use hyperlinks to relevant web pages to offer additional information
- make clear what you want the recipient to do – and why
- avoid using 'text-speak' like LOL or BTW.

TIP *As a rule, always deliver:*

- *good news in writing*
- *bad news verbally, ideally face to face.*

Summary

Effective communication is vital to our success at work, but we can spend too much time communicating at the cost of actually getting things done. Today we learned that by saying more with fewer words we improve our time management. By communicating more concisely and precisely, we convey our message with greater clarity and meaning.

We have learned ways not only to save time when speaking face to face and when using the phone but also in our writing. Short sentences with simple words always work best. Not everyone is a confident reader, but you really can make your writing easy to understand without being patronizing.

Lastly, we looked at how to cope with the flow of emails. Email can be hugely distracting and many of us wrestle with it every day. Managing our inbox using the advice from today is one of the most productive ways there is of improving our time management.

Over the past few days we've covered all the key aspects of good time management. Tomorrow it's time to wrap up with a compendium of useful shortcuts.

SUNDAY

MONDAY

TUESDAY

WEDNESDAY

THURSDAY

FRIDAY

SATURDAY

Fact-check (answers at the back)

1. At work, how should we communicate?
   a) Quietly ❏
   b) By being specific and purposeful ❏
   c) By making sure we aren't caught chatting ❏
   d) By talking to everyone ❏

2. What will using jargon and industry acronyms in a work conversation do?
   a) Impress others with your depth of knowledge ❏
   b) Show people that they aren't as bright as you are ❏
   c) Confuse and possibly alienate the person you're talking to ❏
   d) Remind you what they all mean or stand for ❏

3. When you meet someone important, it's useful to be able to say briefly who you are, what you do and why you are worth talking with further. What is this called?
   a) An elevator pitch ❏
   b) A staircase pitch ❏
   c) Showing off ❏
   d) A washbasin pitch ❏

4. Why is it harder to get your message across on the phone than face to face?
   a) The person you're talking to might not hear too well ❏
   b) It might be a bad line and you could be cut off ❏
   c) Neither of you can read the other's body language ❏
   d) You can't tell what else they're doing while talking to you ❏

5. How could you come over as more businesslike and focused on the phone?
   a) Put your feet on the desk and relax ❏
   b) Close your eyes and imagine you can see the other person ❏
   c) Read their website or LinkedIn profile as you speak ❏
   d) Stand up ❏

6. When you write, what should you always try to do?
   a) Be yourself and write largely as you would speak ❏
   b) Be more formal ❏
   c) Make it impersonal as you're writing on behalf of your organization ❏
   d) Be chatty and familiar ❏

7. When writing, what is the maximum length your sentences should ideally be?
   a) 6 words ❏
   b) 12 words ❏
   c) 18 words ❏
   d) 24 words ❏

8. When should you ideally check your emails?
   a) As soon as the 'ping' tells you they've arrived ❏
   b) Every ten minutes ❏
   c) Every hour, when you pause for a break ❏
   d) Daily ❏

97

9. What is the longest an email should ideally be?
a) 50 words ☐
b) 100 words ☐
c) 150 words ☐
d) 200 words ☐

10. What is the best way to deliver bad news or a complaint?
a) By registered letter ☐
b) By email ☐
c) By putting a poster on the office noticeboard ☐
d) Face to face ☐

SATURDAY

Time management favourites

We started the week by focusing on you, your aspirations and your goals. How can your career deliver these? It's important to know why you're striving to get more done and manage your time better. You had to be motivated to work at the techniques in this book.

So far, we've looked at your job, your workspace, your time, your colleagues and finally your communication. That pretty much covers all the bases. What we've not done yet is explore some of the less obvious, perhaps even quirky, things you can do to boost your time efficiency.

This chapter is different from what you've read thus far. It highlights some of the specific time management tips that work for me. I think they'll probably be useful for you too. They may make you frown, smile and then say 'Aha!'

By the end of today you will:

- have considered my own top time management tips
- feel more in control of your life, work and your time
- see how technology can help you.

Reduce stress

I don't know about you, but I get very wound up sometimes. The truth is that we all suffer from stress to some extent. In many workplaces you see the organization's challenges convert into unrealistic goals. Each person in the chain of command simply divides up then delegates the unrealistic goals further down the line. This creates a situation where everyone blames everyone else for the inevitable failure – except, that is, the unfortunate people at the bottom who have no one to blame.

> **'Why does it take me nearly two hours just to get through the morning emails? Pah, poo and pants.'**
>
> Stephen Fry (Tweet, 18.04.09)

One of my pet hates is people dumping stress on others less able to deal with it than they are. Here's how you can stop people dumping their stress on you when they try to delegate jobs with unrealistic goals.

- Ask how your manager came to accept such a tough challenge.
- Offer to help, but don't accept responsibility or make it your problem.
- Retain control of your diary so that others can't fill it brim full with commitments.
- Make time to exercise, even if it's using the stairs rather than the lift.
- If your health starts to suffer, ease off and look after yourself. You're of no use to anyone if you become ill.

However much you love your job, remember that you are responsible *to* your boss, not responsible *for* them. Don't take on what you know cannot be delivered.

Learn to say no

I've got to know the now retired management writer Charles Handy. Before we first met, I had to persuade his wife it was worth while for him to meet me. She had a reputation for being hard to get past and very protective of her husband's time. When I met him, I realized why. He's such a lovely chap he finds it really difficult to say no. Liz, his wife, acts as gatekeeper and says no for him.

I also find it hard to say no. Too often I find myself helping people with things I frankly should not have got involved with. It could be that you are something of a soft touch too. It's all too easy to sell yourself the idea of helping someone else. The danger is that you end up helping them and neglect your own work as a result.

Try these ways to say no without hurting anyone's feelings.

- 'I'm sorry, but I have a big workload and simply have no capacity for more.'
- 'I'm pretty busy, but if you could send me a short email saying exactly what you want and how you feel I can help, I'll take a look at it.'
- 'I really don't think I'm the right person for this. Why don't you ask...'

As a rule, the longer you delay saying no, the harder it is to do. Get tough.

I'LL HAVE TO HURRY YOU — THE BUILDING'S ON FIRE AND THE FLAMES ARE LICKING AT MY DESK...

Deal with tiredness

We all get tired, particularly if we are trying to pack a lot into our lives. It's one of the problems people encounter when they are studying while working. It's also a problem if you are trying to keep up with people far younger and fitter than you.

Being tired reduces your work rate. I sometimes find myself staring at my computer screen but doing nothing. That's a sign that it's time to switch off and take a break. Here are some effective ways to keep alert at work.

- **Drink water**
  I always have water on my desk and drink lots.

- **Eat fruit**
  I also have fruit on my desk as a great, non-fattening energy boost.

- **Move about**
  I rarely sit still for too long. When I need to think, I pace about; it gets the blood flowing.

- **Sleep well**
  I'm an early bird, so refuse to stay up late at night. I need my full eight hours of sleep and make sure I always get it.

● Keep fit

I am in my mid-fifties, but I run, go the gym and am reduced to a sweating wreck every Saturday by my personal trainer. Fitness gets more important as you get older.

Tiredness can also be a symptom of stress. Understand why you're tired, and then you can do something about it.

Question well

I had the advantage of formal sales training early in my career. This taught me how to control the flow of a conversation. The techniques help me encourage people to tell what I'm trying to find out. It also makes it easier for me to get their commitment. Consequently, I am often well informed and usually persuasive.

Here's how you do this.

Open questions

Open questions make it easy for people to give you information. For example, 'How has your time management improved since you read my book?' Open questions require more than just a yes/no answer.

You direct the question towards the subject you want to hear about. This is great when trying to gather information. It's also a good way to get your children to tell you about their day. Here are two options.

● 'How was school today?' will probably receive the answer 'OK.'
● 'What did you do at school today?' will probably receive a longer answer.

You can focus your open questions by 'funnelling' the person you're talking with towards the area you're most interested in. For example, 'That's really interesting; can you tell me more about the green ones?'

Closed questions

Closed questions enable you to check understanding or gain commitment. They encourage yes/no answers. In sales, they often offer two alternatives, neither of which is no. For example, 'Can we meet to discuss this on Monday at ten, or is Tuesday afternoon better for you?'

Imagine you are delegating a task. You've explained what has to be done and by when. By asking open and closed questions you can make absolutely certain the person understands what it is you want them to do.

- Open question: 'Can you tell me in your own words what it is you are going to do?'
- Closed question: 'And you are confident you can complete the task by Thursday?'

Minutes, not hours

Most people arrange meetings to start at the top of an hour, say at ten o'clock. Diary systems block out time in full hours, so you all sit down expecting to be there for a full hour. The meeting stretches to fill the time available. I like to start meetings at odd times – say, quarter to the hour – and schedule them to finish at quarter or half past. You'd be surprised how much faster a meeting flows when time is limited.

Do it now!

I sometimes shock consultancy clients. When they tell me a client is not buying from them and they don't know why, I ask for their number and ring them there and then. It's so much easier to do things when they're on your mind. Leave stuff until later and you may struggle to make sense of your notes.

Challenging or embarrassing things are almost always better done straight away. Of course, there are some things for which you need to prepare, so please don't become impulsive. However, you'll find plenty of situations where it's timelier to do something immediately than to delay. Here are some good office examples.

- Always keep a spare loo roll beside the toilet. Replace the spare when you start the last roll, not when someone has used the last square.
- Keep spare toner cartridges and, again, replace them when they are fitted, not when you run out.
- When you see that things need to be forwarded to someone else, do it straight away. Don't put stuff down only to pick it up again.
- If you drive a lot, fill up with fuel when the level drops below a quarter full. Then you won't be in a rush when the dial hits red.

Sleep on it

We all face conundrums from time to time at work – the challenges for which there is no clear-cut answer. They can take hours to work out and, even then, you are rarely sure you have made the right decision.

I tend to summarize the possible options on a piece of paper and take it home. I read it late in the evening and start my brain ticking. It's surprising how often I wake in the morning with an answer I've not thought of before.

I'm no neuroscientist, so I don't know how sleeping on challenges works. All I know is that it does. I think it's because my subconscious mind whirrs away at it through the night. Doubtful? Give it a try and see if it works for you.

Talk as you drive

I changed my car recently. Now I can plug my phone into the car and make calls without taking my hands from the steering wheel during the one or two long car journeys I make a week, thus combining the two tasks.

I also always have a list of people I want to talk to, when I can find the time. What I do is arrange phone calls with them in advance, booked at 30-minute intervals, for the duration of my planned journey. Immediately after each call, I phone my office to list what's been agreed. Because I have a very able assistant, sometimes the actions I've agreed have been done before I complete my journey.

Work on trains

I only drive when it's not possible to use the train. Trains can be great places to get some work done. Surrounded by people, you can't really make work phone calls. Internet access is usually sporadic so you're less distracted by email.

Rail journeys enable me to do quality writing without distraction. Sections of this book were written on train journeys. I also try to travel off peak and book my tickets in advance. Often this enables me to travel first class at a lower fare than the regular standard class fare. And finally, pre-booked tickets mean no queuing at the station!

Use visual filing

You've already read about the importance of keeping your office neat and tidy. However, one exception to the minimal paperwork rule that I allow myself is a row of plastic trays in one corner of my office. Each is labelled with a day of the week. I put in these trays anything I know I need to do the next time that day comes round. I also drop in things that come in that I can't deal with or dump straight away. This means little waits more than a week to be done.

Summary

Today we covered several varied time management tips. You may not find them in other time management books, because they are less obvious but still useful time management ideas that you can apply in all areas of your life. It is Saturday after all, a day when most people step back from the weekday toil and think about other aspects of their life.

Some of these tips took us back to the subject of you and your well-being. You are not a machine, and do get tired, upset and stressed. Equally, you have a remarkable brain that can work away on problems when you are asleep. Time management always comes back to you, your motivation, determination and commitment.

Only you can change you. It's easy to blame others for the predicaments we find ourselves in. Often we unwittingly project on to others responsibility for what we actually do to ourselves. And that really does bring us back to the beginning. Only you know what you want to be and how work can help you get there. Take time to know yourself and then the tips in this book will be far easier to put into action. Good luck!

SUNDAY

MONDAY

TUESDAY

WEDNESDAY

THURSDAY

FRIDAY

SATURDAY

Fact-check (answers at the back)

1. When we lose control of what we are committed to, how can we reduce our stress?
   a) Challenge those who ask you to do what looks impossible ❑
   b) Get plenty of sleep before you attempt the impossible ❑
   c) Make sure people know it's not your fault ❑
   d) Cry when you want to get your own way ❑

2. If you find it impossible to say no, what should you do?
   a) Ignore people when they ask you things ❑
   b) Say yes and live with your shortcoming ❑
   c) Get someone else to say no for you ❑
   d) Work harder to get it all done ❑

3. What is the best way to deal with tiredness at work?
   a) Ignore it and plough on regardless ❑
   b) Have a nap and hope the boss doesn't catch you ❑
   c) Drink water, eat fruit or take a quick walk ❑
   d) Vow to party less in future ❑

4. What can using open and closed questions help you do?
   a) Trick people into doing what you want ❑
   b) Maintain control of a conversation ❑
   c) Be really annoying ❑
   d) Get a date with that nice boy/girl in the next office ❑

5. When is the worst time to start a meeting?
   a) Half past the hour ❑
   b) Quarter past the hour ❑
   c) Five to the hour ❑
   d) On the hour ❑

6. What should you do after putting the last loo roll in the holder at work?
   a) Be glad someone put a spare in the room ❑
   b) Use what you want, then hide the rest as a joke ❑
   c) Not even think about this stuff as it's not part of your job ❑
   d) Replace the spare before you go ❑

7. If you go to sleep thinking about a particular work conundrum, what will happen when you wake up?
   a) You'll feel tired ❑
   b) You'll find you've overslept ❑
   c) You'll have some surprising answers to your conundrum ❑
   d) You won't get to sleep at all ❑

8. What's the best way to spend a long work car journey?
   a) Try to arrive ahead of your satnav's prediction ❑
   b) Listen to music and chill out ❑
   c) Have some scheduled phone calls that you can make hands-free ❑
   d) Eat lots of boiled sweets ❑

9. What are train journeys great for?

a) Reading or writing without being distracted ☐
b) People watching ☐
c) Chatting to strangers ☐
d) Sleeping ☐

10. If you have a box file for every day of the week, what should you put in it?

a) A daily treat ☐
b) Your newspaper ☐
c) Stuff you need to get done on that day ☐
d) Nothing ☐

Surviving in tough times

Time really is the final frontier. You cannot make each day longer, yet in these challenging times you have more to do. The solutions to this conundrum can be found in this book. It won't show you how to make time; that's impossible. Instead, it will show you how to make the very best use of the time you have. At a time when everyone's dumping more work on your desk, this book will help you control the flow and conquer the growing pile.

When time is your final frontier, this book will take you to victory!

1 Know where you're heading

It's obvious, really: if you don't know where you're heading, you'll never stick to the best route. At work, now more than ever, if you don't have a clear vision of what's important to your future, you'll not be focused. If you're not focused, you can't prioritize. If you can't prioritize, you'll waste time doing things that are more important to others than to you. This book will help you focus on what's important. Then you can reject the rest!

2 Work when you are most effective

If you don't like Mondays, why not work from Tuesday to Saturday? We all work better on certain days, and we may be at our most productive in the morning or late at night. In our fast-changing and sometimes depressing world, we need to spend our time working when we will be most effective. In tough times, economic problems won't be solved if we stick to the tired old nine to five routine. There's no doubt that, if we all worked when we are at our best, the world would not be in quite such a mess.

3 Toughen up and hunker down

There is no better moment to get organized than now, when everyone is under pressure. Your workspace may be in order and you may be doing much of what this book suggests, but as soon as you pop to the coffee machine, people may be dumping yet more tasks on that nice tidy desk of yours. Be confident and stick to your guns. Hand back what's not really yours and then hunker down and do what's most important to you.

4 Enough is good enough: get real

Everyone admires perfection, but it comes at a price. Right now you've not got time to waste, so make sure your work is good enough – plus a bit. It's like cleaning your car. You can pay at the car wash for a pretty good job, or spend all day Saturday polishing the wheels. Will people notice the wheels? No, and it's the same with those time-consuming embellishments you add to your work tasks.

5 Don't sit on the fence

Indecision hurts. When you have two or more options you need to pick the right one. The fact is that often there is no right or wrong, simply better or worse. This book has helped you become more decisive and that means you can spend your time doing rather than pondering. Procrastination is a time killer. Don't let it make you a victim!

6 Keep your desk tidy

A cluttered desk will clutter your mind. With more to do and change the only constant, you need a clear desk and a clear mind more than ever. Tip out the rubbish from the drawers you never open and start a system. At a time when many are hiding behind piles of files and mountains of documents, you'll stand out from the crowd if you stay neat and tidy. Be tidy and people know you're on top of your job. That'll help you keep it, at a time when everyone around you may well be losing theirs.

7 Get smarter

We all are under pressure right now, so make sure you define each task. It has to be Specific, Measurable, Achievable, Relevant and Timed. If you don't nail these down at the start, your workload will grow before your eyes. You won't know what 'enough' looks like, you won't know where the boundaries are and, worse, without a deadline the problem will go on and on. When everyone's more stressed, working SMART will help you keep your cool.

8 Remember Pareto

He's the guy who pointed out that 20 per cent of our effort delivers 80 per cent of the results. The rest just gets in the way. Peel off the 20 per cent that delivers little and holds you up. Focus on what delivers the goods and delegate or dump as much of the rest as you can.

9 Don't let time thieves steal your success

These are the people who roll up at your desk or drop into your inbox ready for a chat. Worse are the ones with time to kill and a meeting with you in their diary. You know that meetings need agendas and agendas need target times for the completion of each item. You've got work to do and a crisis to conquer. Don't let people with nothing to do drag you down.

10 Be human: it helps

You're not a machine. You get tired, hungry, stressed and sometimes under the weather. This book has shown you how to pace yourself and be realistic. Be kind to yourself and others will follow suit. Remember that those who appear invincible rarely are. Time and today's frantic struggle to keep above water will surely take them under. Be you, love yourself and stay ready to handle the challenges and respond to the opportunities that are sure to come your way.

Answers

Sunday: 1a; 2c; 3b; 4c; 5a; 6d; 7b; 8c; 9c; 10a.

Monday: 1b; 2a; 3c; 4a; 5d; 6b; 7d; 8a; 9c; 10d.

Tuesday: 1a; 2b; 3b; 4c; 5d; 6c; 7c; 8a; 9b; 10a.

Wednesday: 1b; 2a; 3a; 4c; 5d; 6c; 7b; 8a; 9b; 10d.

Thursday: 1c; 2c; 3a; 4c; 5d; 6b; 7b; 8c; 9d; 10d.

Friday: 1b; 2c; 3a; 4c; 5d; 6a; 7b; 8c; 9c; 10d.

Saturday: 1a, 2c; 3c; 4b; 5d; 6d; 7c; 8c; 9a; 10c.

Notes

ALSO AVAILABLE IN THE 'IN A WEEK' SERIES

BODY LANGUAGE FOR MANAGEMENT • BOOKKEEPING AND ACCOUNTING • CUSTOMER CARE • SPEED READING • DEALING WITH DIFFICULT PEOPLE • EMOTIONAL INTELLIGENCE • FINANCE FOR NON-FINANCIAL MANAGERS • INTRODUCING MANAGEMENT • MANAGING YOUR BOSS • MARKET RESEARCH • NEURO-LINGUISTIC PROGRAMMING • OUTSTANDING CREATIVITY • PLANNING YOUR CAREER • SUCCEEDING AT INTERVIEWS • SUCCESSFUL APPRAISALS • SUCCESSFUL ASSERTIVENESS • SUCCESSFUL BUSINESS PLANS • SUCCESSFUL CHANGE MANAGEMENT • SUCCESSFUL COACHING • SUCCESSFUL COPYWRITING • SUCCESSFUL CVS • SUCCESSFUL INTERVIEWING

For information about other titles in the series, please visit
www.inaweek.co.uk

ALSO AVAILABLE IN THE 'IN A WEEK' SERIES

For information about other titles in the series, please visit www.inaweek.co.uk